Like It Is

About the Author

Philip Lyons lives in Bristol and is the author of two pamphlet collections, *Borrowed Time* (Ozymandias Press, 1995) and *Rainy Day* (Loxwood Stoneleigh, 2003). His poems have appeared in magazines and have been broadcast on the radio, and his public readings have included the Wells Festival of Literature and Thornbury Arts Festival. He has taught in universities and prisons, as well as running creative writing groups in a variety of settings. He has also worked as a healthcare assistant, a counsellor, a careers adviser, and a support worker for the long-term unemployed. Since 2007 he has presented a weekly country music show on a community radio station in Bristol, and he was commissioned to write a poem for the University of Bristol's centenary in 2009.

Like It Is

Philip Lyons

Poetry Space Ltd

Like It Is

First published in Great Britain in 2011 by Poetry Space Ltd

© Philip Lyons 2011

Poetry Space Ltd Company No 7144469
Registered office:
21 Davis Close, Barrs Court, Bristol BS30 7BU
www.poetryspace.co.uk

Cover photograph © Chris Sims

Printed and bound in Great Britain
by Whitehall Printing Company Ltd, Bristol

ISBN 978-0-9565328-5-5

For Penny and Jo

Earth's the right place for love:
I don't know where it's likely to go better.

Robert Frost, "Birches"

Contents

Acknowledgements

Acknowledgements are due to the editors of the following publications where some of these poems first appeared: *Bristol Review of Books*, *Candelabrum*, *Orbis* and *Thumbscrew*.

Some of these poems appeared previously in *Borrowed Time* (Ozymandias Press, 1995) and *Rainy Day* (Loxwood Stoneleigh, 2003).

"Marlboro Country" was included in *It's Her Voice That Haunts Me Now: Poems from the Literary Review* (Richard Cohen Books, 1996), edited by Dariane Pictet.

"Growing Pains" was included in *The Winding Road: Family Treasury of Poems and Verses* (Hawthorn Press, 2004), compiled by Matthew Barton.

"A Balm for All Wounds" appeared at the end of a chapter on Paul Celan and Etty Hillesum in *Awake to God: Explorations in the Mystical Way* (SPCK, 2006) by Melvyn Matthews.

"Way Out" was a runner-up in the TLS/Poems on the Underground Poetry Competition 1996 and was published in the booklet of prizewinning poems.

I would like to thank Matthew Barton and Jeremy Mulford for their invaluable help in the arrangement of this collection, as well as for their considered responses to individual poems. I would also like to thank Jane Lyons for her careful reading of the final manuscript.

Aubade

There is a moment when the song begins,
when light peels back the darkness and I sing,
when leaf by leaf the tree assumes its shape,
when I reclaim my throne within its crown.

I sing because the lifeforce tells me to,
because there is so little time to sing,
because my heart is full and fit to burst,
because... because I must, because I can.

You wake to hear me, drowsing in your bed.
You wake and think of how you woke before,
awake in darkness, everything quite still,
awake and waiting for the night to end.

You fall asleep and I become your dream,
become the music you are following,
become a forest where a river flows,
become a glade where you can rest at last.

There is a moment when the song begins.

Borrowed Time

You must be sleeping now, breathing
lightly as the rain attends the land.
Soon you will awake, betrothing
your talents to a cold morning and
cursing it for calling you from your bed.
You were the only alarm I needed.

Even a husbanded heart can smother;
anything less than love would not
survive. A lone wolf in another
country, I am waiting for what
you have already enjoyed: sleep:
counting the cost for want of sheep.

Rainy Day

The rain falls as a blessing or a curse.
I press my lips on yours and drink you in
while beads of water gather on your skin,
each one a microscopic universe.

And who cares if it rains until we drown,
there is no world to come but only this,
eternity compressed into a kiss
before the ticking minutes pull us down.

The boats rock in the harbour. Your eyes glow.
It eases off; the clouds begin to part,
the fragment of blue sky a work of art.
We both have homes to go to and must go.

Country and Western

Tonight I'm putting on my cowboy boots
and going back to Texas for a while,
the prairies where a cowboy has his roots.
I'll lie beneath the stars and smoke cheroots.
This terraced house I live in cramps my style.

My sweetheart doesn't understand. She sighs
and tells me everything I need's at home.
She's frightened of the distance in my eyes.
But I see open plains and endless skies,
and nothing else will still this urge to roam.

I'll only be away a month or two.
You probably won't notice I've been gone,
but don't come looking for me if you do.
I'm going where a cowboy can be blue.
It's something cowboys have to do alone.

Marlboro Country

The lonesome plain. A horse between my knees,
I made my way across the Great Divide.
The doctor told me it was lung disease,
the girl I left behind said suicide –
but either way the fact is that I've died.

So here I am in Marlboro Country, Hell,
where everyone's a cowboy, yes sirree,
and no one minds the suffocating smell
except the sheriff, man we call Big C,
who minds most everything, it seems to me.

I'd be in Heaven if it weren't for God
insisting that all smoking there be banned.
I thought St Peter'd given me the nod,
but then he saw the lit one in my hand.
I told him Marlboro was my favorite brand.

It cut no ice. *To Hell with you,* he said.
I count myself real fortunate indeed
to wind up with these rugged men instead
of with the angels. We're a dying breed,
and dying for a smoke get what we need.

Sometimes She's Past Caring and Sometimes He's Passed Out

Tammy hid the car keys so George rode
the lawnmower into town instead
to buy more booze. "Stand by Your Man"
became "D-I-V-O-R-C-E".
There's only so much a woman can
put up with. Still, George quit drinking
for a while, but when he hit the bottle
again he also hit a bridge. Nearly died.
Tammy went before him through ill health.
You might say there's no justice in the world.
But listen to George sing. It's like the scent
of flowers after rain, both sweet and sad.
>   *The only thing I know to say*
>   *It's been a good year for the roses.*

A Reprieve

Marilyn is walking on the shore,
a star off-duty, mortal for a while,
desiring only this and nothing more:
the sea, the sky, her husband at her side.
She chats with fishermen or jumps the tide,
no cameras flashing, forcing her to smile.

If only it could always be like this!
But then she sees, contorted on the beach,
the fishermen's abandoned, worthless fish
and runs to save each one before the air
consumes it, while the fishermen just stare.
She's in a place her husband cannot reach

although he draws her back across the sand,
distracting her with talk of her next role,
the screenplay he will write for her, the land
where they will build a house, the life
they can look forward to as man and wife.
A seagull swoops and swallows one fish whole.

The Innocent

The organ-grinder plays his droning song
and dressed in infants' clothes I dance along.

I dance although my feet hurt; there's a chance
the man will feed me better if I dance.

The children laugh, too young to recognise
the world's a snare. I tell them with my eyes,

but they are taught by parents not to see
and so they make a monkey out of me.

Resettlement 1944

On 20 February, the Germans had inspected the camp with care and had publicly and loudly upbraided the Italian commissar for the defective organization of the kitchen service and for the scarce amount of wood distributed for heating; they even said that an infirmary would soon be opened. But on the morning of the 21st we learned that on the following day the Jews would be leaving. All the Jews, without exception. Even the children, even the old, even the ill. Our destination? Nobody knew. We should be prepared for a fortnight of travel. For every person missing at the roll-call, ten would be shot.

Primo Levi, *If This Is a Man*

Our last day in the camp, a watery sun
looked down on us like an unseeing eye;
a cold wind blew. There were things to be done,
food got ready for the journey ahead,
washing hung out on the barbed wire to dry,
our cases packed, the children scrubbed and fed.

A silence fell when it was time to leave –
a moment, you could almost say, of prayer,
though if we prayed it was as those who grieve
and not a sign of God's grace in this camp,
the train about to take us who knows where,
the children in clean clothes still slightly damp.

A Balm for All Wounds

We should be willing to act as a balm for all wounds.
                                        Etty Hillesum (October 1942)

The scent of jasmine was her favourite smell.
In Amsterdam it wafted on the breeze.
...and still life will be beautiful, she wrote,
always beautiful. Impassive trees
in line along the edge of the canal.
The gliding motion of a narrowboat.

From within the barbed wire of the place
they sent her to, she watched a soldier pick
wild flowers, herself a lily of the field
to reassure the frightened and the sick
by staying calm. She took her leave with grace
and wrote these words although the truck was sealed:

We left the camp singing.

Brief Encounter

There's someone here who means to do me harm.
Midnight on a deserted street; no sound
but traffic in the distance and the pound-
ing of my heart. Even the rain has gone.
I ask him, *Do I know you?* His reply,
You should do, gives the edge to my alarm.
I almost laugh. Who is this stranger I
am forced to own, whose unforgiving stare
is quite enough to scare me to the bone?
He wants my money, and displays the fist
tucked tight till now inside his coat. Bright snags
of knuckleduster dare me to resist.
So much fuss for one small purse – but there,
that's all I have, unless you want some fags.
Contempt, perhaps. Disgust. *I don't smoke....*
I don't remember noticing him go,
as if I'd missed the punchline of a joke,
still reeling from the first, imagined blow.

Old Lag

Banged up with his son he makes it theirs
and, better still, the women can't get in
to nag at them for money or repairs.
The food is shit but his tobacco tin
is full. He rolls another with a grin.

The good life, see, in spite of all I've heard.
He doesn't hold with cons who just complain
or claim they're innocent (the thought's absurd).
You do your time and then go home again.
He takes a drag. Outside it starts to rain.

He'll stay dry enough but I'll get wet.
He laughs, then coughs and offers me a smoke
as if this were a pub and we'd just met,
an everyday encounter, bloke with bloke —
to light up, have a bevvie, share a joke.

Finishing School

That was a bit below the belt, I said.
He didn't bat an eyelid.
                    Sorry, Phil.
Next time I'll punch you in the face instead.
I laughed it off; he bore me no ill will,
though in his time he'd left hard men for dead.

Armed robbery: a phrase to conjure fear:
him and his mate now facing five to ten
and banged up for the whole length of a year
awaiting trial, cutting it as men,
exchanging dirty jokes and dealing gear.

A screw came rattling by like Marley's ghost.
The lesson ended. Doors clanged. Silence fell.
I sat there thinking of my man's riposte
and pictured him alone back in his cell,
not menacing at all just now but lost.

Prison Hospital

Don't turn your back on me, she said and laughed.
Twenty stone at least, I'd guess – like two
of me – a giant locked up with the daft,
from Holloway where she'd attacked a screw.
I noticed then that I was locked up too.

Her wrists had crevices, deep clefts she'd made
with her own hands, like slits in loaves of bread.
She sat and did her homework on first aid
while other women wrote or drew or read.
I don't know what they pay you for, she said.

The walls were painted purple, meant to calm.
I stared at them, as if they might reveal
the secret of what keeps us safe from harm
or how on earth these wounds would ever heal.
But walls are walls, I thought, and steel is steel.

Her Father's Hands

I have her father's hands – same apelike hair –
though mine show fewer signs of wear and tear
and treat her kinder than her father's did.
She holds one for a second, lifts the lid
and tries to read the lifeline written there.

I take it back; we're not supposed to touch.
But she has touched me more than she can know.
Her depthless eyes can only say so much
and when she speaks her words are hard and slow.
Her father's hands will never let her go.

Sometimes she shouts to get us all to hear,
sometimes she's silent, pretending to be dumb.
She walks around the room or sucks her thumb.
She's living on the knife-edge of her fear,
in prison now until the doctors come.

Who Shall Remain Nameless

I call his name. He calls himself The Victim,
staring at me in the underpass
as if I were the devil who had picked him
to walk through fire and swallow broken glass
and not the former teacher of his class

in prison, where he sat uncomprehending
but safe because I simply let him be.
I let him be again – no use pretending
I've anything to give him now he's free.
A homeless busker meanwhile sings off-key,

a sixties tune though he is barely twenty.
I hurry up the steps to daylight, sure
of purpose, confident, the child of plenty,
and head for home where, once I've closed the door,
the world can go to hell. That's what home's for.

Way Out

This street is like an endless corridor
to one who's spent the best part of his life
in hospital. He's looking for the door.
The sun is glinting like a sharpened knife.

It dazzles him; he has to shield his eyes.
He scans the floor for dog-ends, then stops dead.
The voices in his head are telling lies
again: I said, you said, he said, she said.

The driver barely has a chance to brake,
and passers-by are in that instant shocked
by something like the sound a key will make
when being forced to turn a rusty lock.

Two Poems from the Day Hospital

1 The Old Clinic

The ghosts of patients who had ECT
when this was still a clinic haunt the room,
fill it with a weight that can't be moved
however many games we play. They sigh
at times in unison, *We are unloved.*
Please love us, becoming louder in the gloom.

X throws the ball to me and says my name.
I follow suit. It's Monday afternoon.
I sense them all around us looking on
as if they too would like to join the game.
I wonder what they do when we are gone.
Do they imagine we will love them soon?

2 The Top Floor Flat

Come in. Take a pew. As you can see
we're quite informal here. Help yourself to tea
or coffee. Yes, it is a wonderful view.
Oh, dear. Don't worry, we'll soon mop it up.
Everyone gets nervous when they're new.
Go on, pour yourself another cup.
I'll see you later — we can have a chat,
talk about your tablets, things like that.

Flames consume me. My eyes begin to melt.
Inside my head I hear a perfect shriek
but nothing happens when I try to speak.
The skin falls off me in great strips like felt.
Soon I shall be an outline in the air,
a quiver in the light, a coil of smoke
that rises to the ceiling and hovers there,
spreading outwards like an unseen cloak.

Writing Group in the Day Hospital

Each alone yet here together
seeking words for emptiness and pain.
We have so many words for weather
and yet so few that might explain
our inner weather. Words like rain
keep falling but don't stay.
It's not that there is nothing we can say
but words like hope get washed away.

Visiting

A single magpie on the lawn
examining the grass for signs
of worms, bedraggled and forlorn
but nonetheless committed to
survival; flowers in straight lines
now drooping in the rain like patients
who've forgotten how to queue
yet know they have to stand like this
till someone from the nurses' station
comes to give them medicine;
a winding path that may or may
not lead to where I want to go,
depending on which notice I
can trust; a wall; a gate that's locked;
a door that's also locked and so
I press a buzzer – someone lets
me in; a staircase in a block;
a flight of concrete stairs I climb
to find her waiting in a dress
too big and almost out of time.

Asylum

The fear of hell remained and now you're in it.
Even from the outside it looks grim,
with nurses who at best seem quite indifferent
and other women screaming, slamming doors.

I tell you I can only stop a minute.

We sit and listen to the clock tick tock.

You've got so thin your skin's almost transparent.
You sip a cup of water, whisper you
can't swallow, claim your insides are all blocked.

I think of things to say but nothing comes

except a memory of playing shops,
how neatly you arranged your tray, the coins
from every sale kept hidden somewhere safe;
if others squabbled you would take no part.

My sensible big sister, I can't stay.

You reach out for my hand and break my heart.

Bystander

How many years ago was it? – twenty-five? –
I saw you behind the wheel of your yellow Beetle
driving up Kellaway Avenue to Coldharbour Road
and I knew I was seeing my future,
though not endowed with sufficient prophetic gifts
to guess how long that future might last.
When you recognised me standing on the pavement
you grinned and waved, and then were gone.

I don't know why I'm saying this now.
The time we lived together came and went.
The yellow Beetle was the first to go,
then two cars later me,
the man who saw his future driving past.
Perhaps I should have looked the other way.

Rosemary's Green Fingers

Rosemary is at home with potted plants.
She kneads the dark, dank earth – a nest for seeds –
while making light of all her disappointments.
The kettle boils. A garden clear of weeds
confronts me from the window; baize-like lawn.
The neighbours' black cat stalks across the floor
and rubs itself against me as I yawn.
I pour two cups of coffee but ignore
the purring cat until it bites my toe,
Egyptian god demanding sacrifice.
Rosemary's plants are lined up in a row
like refugees with hands held out for rice.

Rosemary fills a watering-can at the sink,
which wakes me up – I must have nodded off.
The sky has turned mellifluously pink.
What right have I to ask for more? I cough
involuntarily – a summer cold –
and make a joke of being so effete
by feigning sudden death. (How very droll.)
The plants outside have withered in the heat.
Rosemary waters them; their leaves unfurl
like scrolls as if to recognise such care,
for Rosemary is a tender-hearted girl;
she urges me to sniff the scented air.

The Garden

The foxes came and went, and even though
you left out plates of dog food they would not
survive, their mangy frames a little worse
each time we watched them crossing the back wall.
A lesson, then, in natural selection:
defeated by disease and wheelie bins,
these visitors who'd brought us so much joy.

That summer, when we sat outside, the lawn
seemed empty and the air too pure; we missed
the pungent smell of fox. At night we lay
apart and listened for their mating cries
in vain. The apples ripened on the tree,
their plumpness witness to the recent rain.
We stayed indoors and left them where they fell.

Leaving Home

She says I've left her
with nothing. I say she's kept
the house and the car
but she says
that's not what she meant.

We're sitting at her table
(our table)
the way we always used to sit –
her facing the oven,
me with my back to it.

It's been almost a year.

I've come to pick up some things.

She says I didn't give her
any warning. I say I tried.
I could have tried harder,
she says. I say
I'm sorry.

When I get up to leave
she follows me to the hall.
We hug briefly,
her parting shot
You're not coming home then?

Like It Is

It's like the nightingale we stood and listened to
together. The wood at dusk. The other birds
becoming silent. The stillness in the air.
The brief, intoxicating sense that life
was good. The slow appearance of the stars.
The journey home. The promise of renewal there.

It's like the day you asked me *Is there someone else?*
The walk we were on. The pleasant lunch we'd had
at a country pub. The view across the plain.
The buzzard circling calmly overhead
in a demonstration of perfect poise.
The intermittent sunshine. The slight chance of rain.

Elegy

No sentimental last goodbye. No tears.
So little I could say these past ten years
that didn't make you have a fit of pique.
You won't be anything but ash next week.
I shan't be there, of course. I will behave
(don't want you turning in your virtual grave
the moment you arrive). No tears, I swear.

But if they fall it's neither here nor there
like drizzle on a summer's day or dew
(remembering the wealth of flowers you grew)
and if you think this might be a farewell
I wouldn't argue with the dead yet tell
you plainly, as I watch the sky turn grey,
you're with me like a ghost who plans to stay.

Moving On

The house I left behind was sold last year,
its contents doubtless bagged and thrown away
apart from stuff like books and furniture.
I think *What happened to the photos, say,*
I took that first time in Ravello? Views
of mountains, the piazza, lemon trees:
a record of those moments I refuse
to disregard though they no longer please.

Our second trip to the Amalfi coast
I ditched the camera, wanting to retain
the essence of each day as it was lived.
It makes no difference now; what's lost is lost.
I can't say I was wrong to cause you pain
and you can't say there's nothing to forgive.

Unread

1

I know you can't be reading this, as sure
as two and two make four, though what I know
is questionable at best. I'm letting go
and you're a balloon that's floating to a dot.
I watch you closely till you disappear.
I'm here (a little worse for wear); you're not.

I carry round your anger in my gut,
a grating voice that tells me I have sinned,
when all I've done is free you to the wind
and say goodbye. I held on long enough.
You can't be reading this, I'm sure of that,
but if you are I wrote these words with love.

2

I wrote these words with love, but if you are
at all unsure (*I love you too*, you said,
whatever that might mean) I'll write instead,
although you can't be reading this: I think
about you at the bus stop, in the car,
at work, when walking, standing at the sink,

and every time it's like a hand has found
its way inside my chest to squeeze my heart
and won't let go. You trusted me. That's hard
to make a poem out of or ignore,
especially when you are in the ground,
not reading this, not reading this, I'm sure.

Cold Comfort

You wouldn't want to be alive today.
You wouldn't want to go out in the sleet
that's tumbling through a sky of charcoal grey
to chill your bones. You wouldn't want your feet
to have the blood starved from them in a bid
to keep your vitals warm. You wouldn't want
to scrape ice off the car only to skid
into a tree outside the office, planted
at your request some years before.
                                    But then
again you always made the best of things,
a stoic even when your heart was sore,
and though I'm not the faithfulest of men
I try to do the same. Your absence stings.
The sleet has turned to rain and starts to pour.

Gabriel

I remember my astonishment the time
we were walking in a group by the canal
and you stripped down to your underpants and swam –
you, the otherworldly intellectual,
in that filth! But water was your element.
Your physique was surprisingly muscular
and you swam with great strength. I was torn between
admiration and fear of what you might catch
in there. Over the years we lost touch. I heard
you became ill. Not from the water. Cancer.
In the end it killed you, a man in his prime
still. My mind goes blank. What else is there to say?
All I can think of is you in that canal,
those powerful strokes, us walking alongside.

The View from Here

Each year the rocks come loose and fall like crumbs
into the gorge. The earth will not be still.
I look down on the traffic scuttling by
and think of how you stood here in the dark
already turning into stone, so cold
that bleak December night the river froze.
Be still, we said, and then your heart came loose.
The wonder was you had endured so long.

I come here empty-handed, knowing time
itself won't heal this gaping wound, this rift,
yet come here all the same to talk to you,
to stand with you awhile on shifting ground
and share what's left of what you left behind,
enough at least to keep me holding on.

The Life to Come

Death when we met was disarmingly charming.
He offered me a cigarette and poured me
a drink. *Welcome to Hell,* he said brightly.
*The place has had its critics but I think
you'll really like it here. The Devil's not
so bad once you get to know him – and you will.*

It was a lot to take in. Death continued:
*Of course, I'm happy as your guide to point
out the alternative facilities,
but between you and me they've gone downhill.
The constant change of management hasn't helped.
Your glass is empty; let me top you up.*

I said nothing. *You seem surprised. I guess
I'm not what you expected. The truth is
I got so bored with all that hooded-cloak-
and-scythe Grim Reaper stuff. Pure pantomime.
These days I prefer a more professional
approach. Customer focused, you might say.*

At last I found my voice. I said *Hang on
a minute. Why am I here? I'm still alive.*
Death laughed. *I think that's what we call denial.
But suit yourself, I've all the time in the world.
You may as well have a look, though, while you're here.
I'll get Beelzebub to show you round.*

Amazing Grace

I used to have an aunt called Grace,
as fat as fat can be.
She liked to make a funny face
and gobble up her tea.

She had a husband who was blind –
the joke's not hard to see.
But looking at it now I find
in fact the joke's on me.

For they have gained the other shore
where everyone is free:
no fat, no thin, no rich, no poor.
The dead have dignity.

It cheers me to imagine how
when we come face to face
the seraphim will turn and bow
to honour my aunt Grace.

Sirens

While Ulysses was lashed to the mast I
crept up from the lower deck to find out
what all the fuss was about. There was mist
too thick to see through, though I swear I caught
a glimpse of one, her shock of hair like fire.

Their voices seemed far off at first, a tune
that's half-remembered, something overheard;
then rising falling as the sea itself
their singing filled the air like cinnamon
or oranges when you break them open.

I felt as if they called to me alone.
It was my mother saying *Come on in,*
it's getting dark, my first love saying *Here,*
I'm here. I dived to meet them through the waves,
alive to every possibility.

Infidelity

Her body tasted of the sea, which threw me.
She said *It's just like falling through the sky
and floating free.* I wondered if she knew me.

The morning after when we said goodbye
I did my best to look like I was sad,
performed a ritual kiss, relived the lie

that I was cut out to be Galahad
and not the heel who only days from now
would make her cry. Perhaps I did feel bad,

perhaps I really made a mental vow
to be a better person. All I know
is walking home I stopped to buy some flowers,

a bunch of roses with a big red bow.

Stormy Weather

You send me postcards from Hope Cove.
I count the days till you return
and read between the lines to learn
the progress of our love.

When you come back will you come back
to me or will it be to him?
I close my eyes and watch you swim
beneath a sky turned black.

The sea boils over, waves crash down
and you are dragged far out of reach.
A dog is barking on the beach.
I'm terrified you'll drown.

Best not to dwell on what you write.
I climb up Brandon Hill and see
you sitting where you sat with me
and I am filled with light.

Lunch

I eat the remains of the olive bread
you brought with you yesterday. Do I like
olives? Yes, I do. I love you. The bread
is still soft, pleasingly chewy. I cut
a slice of cheese. *You're not eating much — I
don't have much appetite — Tell me what's wrong.*
I am trying to squeeze myself into
a day that won't fit. I'm wearing the same
jumper you found amusing yesterday.
Lilac. That's very gay, though not on you.
I love you. Would you have stayed if I'd said
I can't live without you, even though it's
not true? It's only the first day. The bread
still tastes new. I love you. I love you. I

The Big Match

We played our best match here in England,
me at home and you away from home.
The ref was biased in your favour though,
I must say, and I was learning to be kind
by squandering the home advantage. Time
and time again I could have taken the lead;
once I even missed an open goal.
Then you broke loose and left me standing, wove
around my flat back four and scored, your fans
still singing as you left the field triumphant.

The return match was a disappointment.
You had found a manager by then
and I was having an indifferent season.
No contest! If I analyse it now
you dominated the midfield, had strength
in depth, won more balls in the air. I should
have used the sweeper system, I suppose,
but that's just being wise after the event.
Home or away, you were the better team
by a mile. No, by a whole continent.

Coda

I listen to the silence. It says love
is not the path to happiness I thought
it was. I light another cigarette.

The silence hasn't finished with me yet.

It says in time I'll learn how to forgive,
relinquish what I've lost, annul the debt,
breathe deeper than before and start to live.

I would have loved you till the day I died,
but my attempt to love you came to naught
and nothing fills me where there once was light.

You took me by surprise and I was caught.

I gave you all I had. It wasn't quite
enough. I raise my glass to better days.
There is an end to this, the silence says.

Come and Meet Me

Come and meet me – I am waiting here.
The light sifts through an avenue of trees
and everything is luminously clear,
so come and meet me. I am waiting here
to share your dreams before they disappear
like pollen carried elsewhere by the breeze.
Come and meet me – I am waiting here.
The light sifts through an avenue of trees.

Autumn Leaves

The leaves are falling. I will try to catch one,
make a wish and hope the wish comes true,
and though they say be careful what you wish for
I'll not hesitate to wish for you.

I love the trees in autumn. How they shake
their heads. Leaves catch the light before they fall.
We fall like leaves and hope someone will catch us
yet know the earth will surely catch us all.

Normally Such a Careful Driver

Two pheasants on a motorway:
one got run over, one got away.

The day of our engagement (before I proposed).
One pheasant flew, the other one froze.

It isn't a symbol; it wasn't a sign.
We're happily married; everything's fine.

But I think of that bird as it bounced off the car
and time seemed to stop. How lucky we are,

wouldn't you say? How lucky we are.

We're

over the moon
    not over the hill,
        not under the weather
            but under a spell.
I think it's called love.
    It's tougher than leather
        but light as a feather
            and sound as a bell.

We're happy as Larry,
    a lark or a king
        to marry each other
            and each wear a ring.
It's definitely love.
    We're in it together
        for now and for ever,
            come winter, come spring.

In the Summerhouse

A wedding present from our friends, it's where
I go to be alone. I watch the sky
and breathe the slowly cooling summer air.

A red and white hot-air balloon floats by,
rising just in time to clear the trees
beyond the line of gardens. Two geese fly

towards the river. Insects surf the breeze.
At dusk the houses come alive with light
and windows hold their contents like a frieze.

There at the sink you peer into the night.
It's too dark now to see me wave. Your face
is luminous, a reassuring sight

to draw me homewards from my hiding-place.

To My Wife Asleep

Years from now when we are both long dead
I hope there'll be an echo of this scene:
a man and woman lying in a bed,
the wife asleep, the husband curled around her,
and in the darkness just the sound of rain.

I lie here trying not to think of work.
Your heart is beating underneath my arm,
your body's warmth a comfort. Worries lurk
inside my skull like coils too tightly wound,
but till the morning they can do no harm.

The world will bark its orders soon enough.
For now I am content to be awake
and know that what I feel for you is love,
the common sort: two human beings bound
together by a bond that does not break.

Growing Pains

(for Jo on her thirteenth birthday)

A clarinet is laughing in a room
upstairs. The rain's set in, a dismal day,
though right outside there is a patch of green
that might just be a metaphor for joy —
the way it's always there despite the pain
if we can see it, waiting to be seen.

You have your mother's way of making friends.
You notice other people. It's a gift,
like being musical or good at sport.
I see you walk towards me on the lawn.
You smile and say you feel much better now.
You find the grass is greener than you thought.

Poem for My Stepdaughter

And you'll always have
What you gave to love

Beth Nielsen Chapman

I'm listening to a song called "Deeper Still"
when you walk in. You find my music sad
and say so once again, then hover till
I give you my attention. I'd be mad
to tell you how the song is really you,
how just by standing there you fill my heart
with joy and make me want to dance. It's true
I listen to sad songs, but life like art
is sometimes sad and this song "Deeper Still"
is beautiful, a song that tells me why
I'm here. I look at you and you say *Phil,*
I have to leave now or I'm going to cry.

Coming of Age

(for Jo on her twenty-first birthday)

You're not my flesh and blood. Your brains, your looks
don't come from me. I didn't watch you grow
or hold your hand the day you started school.

At thirteen there wasn't much you didn't know.
You taught me how to recognise a need
for love and be more loving. In return

I helped you study. Now when you succeed
I feel a father's pride. At twenty-one
you are a woman with both grace and style,

determined, yes, but also kind – a star.
You keep me on my toes. You make me smile.
You tell me it's all good. How right you are.

Anniversary

Wood pigeons have returned to nest
outside our window in the tree
you said reminded you of when
you were a child. The litmus test
of home is where you want to be.
Let's not ever move again.

Relationships that fall apart
from lack of proper husbandry
bring home (or closer to our door)
the danger of a change of heart.
What was he thinking? *You* tell *me*!
One pigeon, patient as before,

sits motionless, content to brood,
untroubled by a dialogue
about our friends' domestic state,
while one has gone in search of food
and down below the neighbours' dog
stands like a sentry at his gate.

Evening Sonnet

Twilight, then nightfall. Stars like grains of salt.
I'm not myself. I pour another Scotch
and settle in the summerhouse to watch
the show. The sky is perfect to a fault,
despite the stars that lie by being seen
when they're not there. An owl begins its cry
as if to glorify creation. Why
am I so out of sorts? Why less serene?

This being human is no easy thing,
to wake each day and know that death is near
yet far enough away to let me think
I might just live for ever. Birds that sing
and stars that shine are bound to disappear.
I'm in the dark. I'm savouring my drink.

The Sun at Burghclere

A grey sky covered us as we entered
the chapel, but though our eyes took a while
to adjust to the deeper grey within,
light through the window brought the walls to life
and with them scenes from Stanley Spencer's war.
Behind the altar, stretching to the roof,
The Resurrection of the Soldiers made
us gasp, soldiers bearing plain white crosses,
a team of dead mules turning towards Christ,
the debris of the battlefield made whole.
We left the place in silence. Birdsong filled
the air. The sun came out, the way it does
sometimes: big show-off source of life, intent
on shining somewhere, dazzling us with light.